National Basketball Association

Author: Rausch, David
Reading Level: 3.4
Point Value: 0.5
Quiz Number: 169999

Accelerated Reader

NATIONAL BASKETBALL ASSOCIATION

BY DAVID RAUSCH

BELLWETHER MEDIA • MINNEAPOLIS, MN

EPIC BOOKS are no ordinary books. They burst with intense action, high-speed heroics, and shadows of the unknown. Are you ready for an Epic adventure?

This edition first published in 2015 by Bellwether Media, Inc.

No part of this publication may be reproduced in whole or in part without written permission of the publisher. For information regarding permission, write to Bellwether Media, Inc., Attention: Permissions Department, 5357 Penn Avenue South, Minneapolis, MN 55419.

Library of Congress Cataloging-in-Publication Data

Rausch, David.
  National Basketball Association / by David Rausch.
    pages cm. – (Epic: Major League Sports)
  Includes bibliographical references and index.
  Summary: "Engaging images accompany information about the National Basketball Association. The combination of high-interest subject matter and light text is intended for students in grades 2 through 7"– Provided by publisher.
  ISBN 978-1-62617-135-0 (hardcover : alk. paper)
  1. National Basketball Association–Juvenile literature. 2. Basketball–History–Juvenile literature. I. Title.
  GV885.515.N37R38 2014
  796.323'64–dc23
                                2014010562

Printed in the United States of America, North Mankato, MN.

TABLE OF CONTENTS

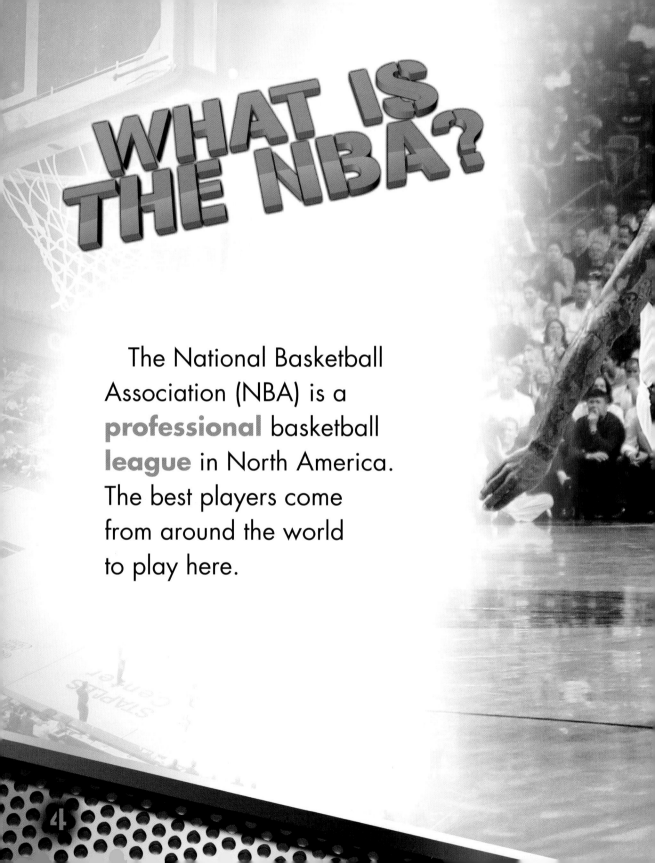

WHAT IS THE NBA?

The National Basketball Association (NBA) is a **professional** basketball **league** in North America. The best players come from around the world to play here.

HISTORY OF THE NBA

The NBA formed in 1949 when the National Basketball League (NBL) **merged** with the Basketball Association of America (BAA). Teams from small towns and large cities joined together.

BAA

CAGERS

Before the NBA formed, players were often called "cagers." The first pro games were played in wire cages.

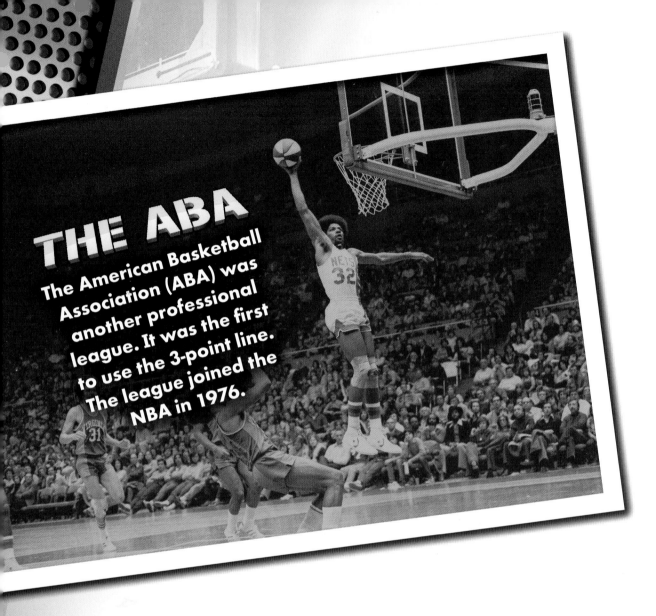

THE ABA

The American Basketball Association (ABA) was another professional league. It was the first to use the 3-point line. The league joined the NBA in 1976.

Before the merge, NBL teams played in gyms and ballrooms in the Midwest. The BAA used large arenas. This attracted the best ball players to the BAA.

A LOOK BACK

1937:   **The National Basketball League forms.**

June 6, 1946:   **The Basketball Association of America forms.**

April 22, 1947:   **The Philadelphia Warriors beat the Chicago Stags to win the first BAA Finals.**

July 1, 1947:   **The first BAA draft is held. Clifton McNeeley is the number one pick.**

August 3, 1949:   **The NBL joins the BAA to become the National Basketball Association.**

March 2, 1951:   **The first NBA All-Star Game is played.**

March 26, 1962:   **Reggie Harding becomes the first high school player to get drafted into the pros.**

February 17, 1968:   **The Basketball Hall of Fame opens its doors in Springfield, Massachusetts.**

August 5, 1976:   **The American Basketball Association joins the NBA.**

July 30, 2005:   **The NBA decides to no longer draft high school players.**

Basketball Hall of Fame

THE TEAMS

The NBA has 30 teams. They play in either the Eastern or Western **Conference**. Each conference has three **divisions** of 5 teams.

EASTERN CONFERENCE

Atlantic
- Boston Celtics
- Brooklyn Nets
- New York Knicks
- Philadelphia 76ers
- Toronto Raptors

Central
- Chicago Bulls
- Cleveland Cavaliers
- Detroit Pistons
- Indiana Pacers
- Milwaukee Bucks

Southeast
- Atlanta Hawks
- Charlotte Hornets
- Miami Heat
- Orlando Magic
- Washington Wizards

WESTERN CONFERENCE

Northwest
- Denver Nuggets
- Minnesota Timberwolves
- Oklahoma City Thunder
- Portland Trail Blazers
- Utah Jazz

Pacific
- Golden State Warriors
- Los Angeles Clippers
- Los Angeles Lakers
- Phoenix Suns
- Sacramento Kings

Southwest
- Dallas Mavericks
- Houston Rockets
- Memphis Grizzlies
- New Orleans Pelicans
- San Antonio Spurs

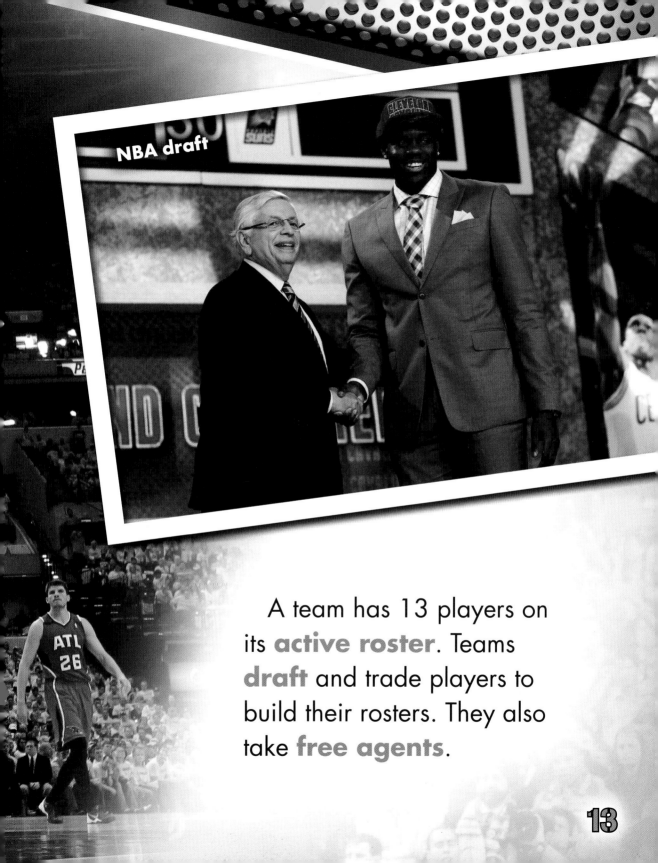

NBA draft

A team has 13 players on its **active roster**. Teams **draft** and trade players to build their rosters. They also take **free agents**.

PLAYING THE GAME

Every game starts with a **tip-off**. Then four 12-minute **quarters** follow. Both teams score by shooting baskets. **Referees** blow their whistles if the rules are broken.

TIE GAME

A tie game goes into overtime. These periods last for 5 minutes. They continue until one ends with a winner.

referee

14

BASKETBALL TALK

2-pointer—when a ball is shot inside the 3-point line; 2 points

3-pointer—when a ball is shot behind the 3-point line; 3 points

block—when a ball is stopped from going in the basket

dribble—when the ball is bounced; players can only move with the ball while dribbling.

field goal—when a basket is scored on a shot other than a free throw; 2 or 3 points

foul—when an illegal action happens on another player; results in a turnover.

free throw—when a player can take a free shot; 1 point

pass—when a player throws the ball to another player

steal—when a player takes the ball from another player

travel—when a player runs or walks with the ball without dribbling; results in a turnover.

turnover—when a player gives the ball to the other team

15

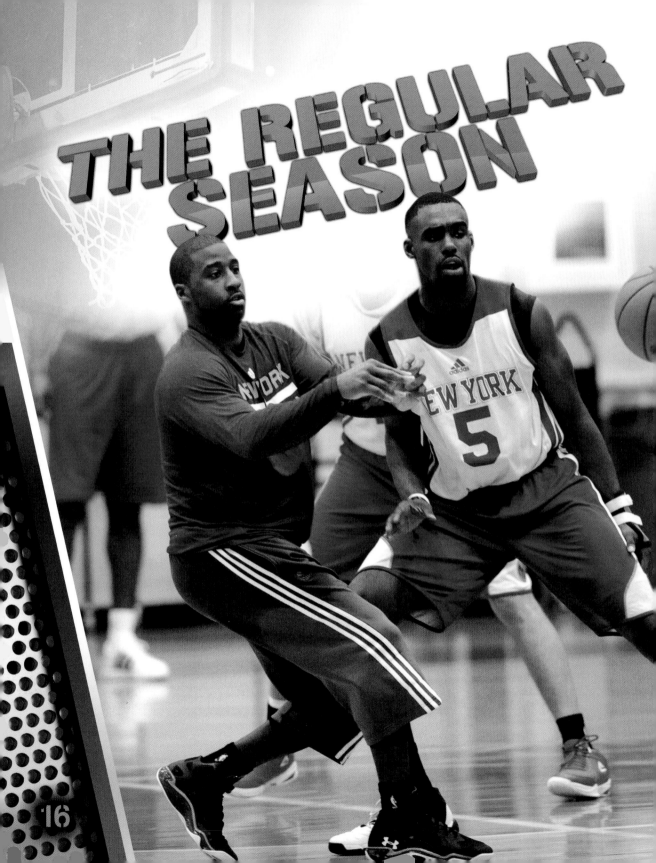

THE REGULAR SEASON

Teams have training camp in September and October. Then their 82-game season starts. In February, the best players go to the **All-Star Game**.

ALL-STAR WEEKEND

All-Star Weekend has many basketball activities. A fan favorite is the Slam Dunk Contest.

THE PLAYOFFS AND THE NBA FINALS

The playoffs start in April. Each conference brings eight teams to the playoffs. There are three rounds to reach the NBA Finals.

The conference champions meet in the NBA Finals. They battle for the Larry O'Brien Championship Trophy. The winning team is crowned NBA Champions!

MVP

A Most Valuable Player award is given for the NBA Finals. Michael Jordan has won the most with six.

Larry O'Brien Championship Trophy

GLOSSARY

active roster—a list of players on a team who can play in an NBA game

All-Star Game—a game between players chosen as the best at their positions; the NBA All-Star Game is between the Eastern and Western Conferences.

conference—a group of sports teams within a league; teams in a conference often play one another.

divisions—groups of sports teams within a conference; teams in a division often play one another.

draft—to choose players from college teams to join the NBA

free agents—professional athletes who are free to play for any team; free agents do not have contracts.

league—a group of people or teams united by a common interest or activity

merged—joined to become one

professional—a level where athletes get paid to play a sport

quarters—the four periods of time in a football or basketball game

referees—people who enforce the rules during a game

tip-off—how a basketball game is started; a referee tosses the ball up between two opposing players.

TO LEARN MORE

At the Library

Coy, John. *Hoop Genius: How a Desperate Teacher and a Rowdy Gym Class Invented Basketball.* Minneapolis, Minn.: Carolrhoda Books, 2013.

De Medeiros, Michael. *NBA.* New York, N.Y.: AV2 by Weigl, 2013.

LeBoutillier, Nate. *Play Basketball Like a Pro: Key Skills and Tips.* Mankato, Minn: Capstone Press, 2011.

On the Web

Learning more about
the National Basketball Association
is as easy as 1, 2, 3.

1. Go to www.factsurfer.com.

2. Enter "National Basketball Association" into the search box.

3. Click the "Surf" button and you will see a list of related web sites.

With factsurfer.com, finding more information is just a click away.

INDEX

The images in this book are reproduced through the courtesy of: Al Diaz/ MCT/ Newscom, front cover (left), p. 21; George Bridges/ Abaca USA/ Newscom, front cover (right); David Santiago/ MCT/ Newscom, pp. 4-5; Associated Press, pp. 6, 7, 8, 12, 16, 17; alexsvirid, p. 9; Ronald Martinez/ Pool/ EPA/ Newscom, p. 10; Jason Szenes/ EPA/ Corbis, p. 13; Brian Kersey/ UPI/ Newscom, p. 14; Larry W. Smith/ EPA/ Newscom, p. 19; Sonia Canada/ Cordon Press/ Corbis, p. 20 (left); Jeff Haynes/ Agence France Presse/ Newscom, p. 20 (right).